GREAT ZIMBABWE

HOUSES OF STONE

ZIMBABWE

AFRICAN PUBLISHING GROUP
PO Box BW 350, Harare
ZIMBABWE

David Martin, Pictures as credited, Maps and Published edition APG

Photographic Credit. Front cover a rainbow over the Hill Complex, back cover a replica of most complete Zimbabwe Bird in front of Conical Tower. All colour pictures David Martin except pages 15, National Gallery of Zimbabwe and 61, Tony Martin. Black and white pictures pages 7, 31, 34, 38, 39, 40, 41, 60, and 63 National Archives of Zimbabwe. Maps Surveyor Generals Department.

ISBN: 0-7974-1665-X

Design: Paul Wade, Ink Spots, Harare

Bardwell Printers

CONTENTS

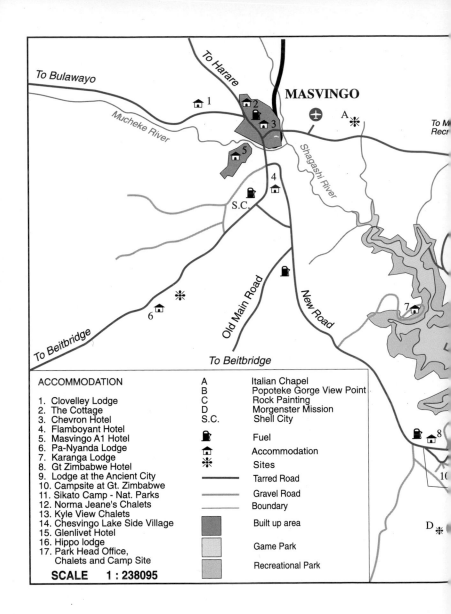

To Bulawayo

To Harare

MASVINGO

Mucheke River

Shagashi River

A

To M
Recr

S.C.

Old Main Road

New Road

To Beitbridge

To Beitbridge

7

8

10

D

ACCOMMODATION

1. Clovelley Lodge
2. The Cottage
3. Chevron Hotel
4. Flamboyant Hotel
5. Masvingo A1 Hotel
6. Pa-Nyanda Lodge
7. Karanga Lodge
8. Gt Zimbabwe Hotel
9. Lodge at the Ancient City
10. Campsite at Gt. Zimbabwe
11. Sikato Camp - Nat. Parks
12. Norma Jeane's Chalets
13. Kyle View Chalets
14. Chesvingo Lake Side Village
15. Glenlivet Hotel
16. Hippo lodge
17. Park Head Office,
    Chalets and Camp Site

SCALE   1 : 238095

A	Italian Chapel
B	Popoteke Gorge View Point
C	Rock Painting
D	Morgenster Mission
S.C.	Shell City

Fuel

Accommodation

Sites

Tarred Road

Gravel Road

Boundary

Built up area

Game Park

Recreational Park

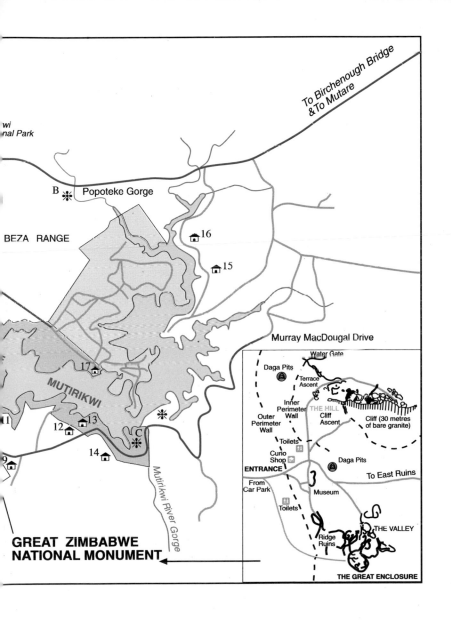

To Birchenough Bridge
&To Mutare

wi
nal Park

B ☀ Popoteke Gorge

BEZA RANGE

🏠16

🏠15

Murray MacDougal Drive

MUTIRIKWI

☀

1
12🏠 🏠13

C ☀

14🏠

9🏠

Mutirikwi River Gorge

**GREAT ZIMBABWE
NATIONAL MONUMENT** ←

Water Gate

Daga Pits
🅰

Terrace
Ascent

Inner
Perimeter
Wall

THE HILL

Cliff (30 metres
of bare granite)

Outer
Perimeter
Wall

Cliff
Ascent

Toilets

Curio
Shop

ENTRANCE

Daga Pits
🅰

To East Ruins

From
Car Park

Museum

Toilets

THE VALLEY

Ridge
Ruins

THE GREAT ENCLOSURE

ACKNOWLEDGEMENTS

I am particularly grateful to Edward Matenga, the senior curator of archaeology based at Great Zimbabwe. He walked and talked me around Great Zimbabwe on several occasions explaining the intricacies of both the monument and of Shona customs and culture.

Kevin Walsh of the University of Zimbabwe, Department of Geology, provided source materials and corrected the draft manuscript. Robert Soper and Godfrey Ncube of the UZ Department of History commented on the draft.

Meg Coates Palgrave provided the trees checklist, Dr Kit Hustler and Peter Ginn the birds checklist. Marguerite MacLean of the Lodge at the Ancient City, Graham and Cally Richards at Pa-Nyanda Lodge and Grant Raubenheimer at the Great Zimbabwe Hotel provided hospitality. Zimbabwe Sun Hotels gave generous financial support to this Guide.

I owe a debt to two members of the African Publishing Group staff, David Mupfurutsa and Kathleen Ginn, who researched the materials for this book and checked the contents.

Finally, I must particularly thank Judy Boyd for editing the manuscript, and my partner and friend, Phyllis Johnson, for her encouragement and expertise as I grappled with the pre-colonial period.

INTO AFRICA TRAVEL GUIDES

This is one of ten area-specific *Into Africa Travel Guide* books on Zimbabwe, aimed at covering the country in depth and showing visitors and residents alike that there is a great deal to be learned and seen in Zimbabwe.

Most of the Guides follow a basic pattern. They begin with geology, followed by archaeology, which allows coverage of the Stone Age. The Iron Age is covered in the pre-colonial section, then the colonial period follows. Thereafter, specific attractions for each area are detailed.

This Guide on Great Zimbabwe is somewhat different from others in the series in that it focuses almost exclusively on the monument. Given the limited number of other attractions in the area, and the deliberate confusion about Great Zimbabwe's origins, this seems appropriate.

David Martin

INTRODUCTION

The word zimbabwe derives from the Shona language: *dzimba dza mabwe* **(houses of stone) or** *dzimba woye* **(venerated houses)**

Whenever I mention to a European that I find the spirits at Great Zimbabwe benign, I am rewarded by one of those looks the English reserve for the eccentric and reminded of the refrain "Mad dogs and Englishmen..."

You may have just such a reaction. A slight, bird-like, lowering of the head to the left, that quizzical, but of course understanding nod. Then a swift retreat.

The emotional reactions evoked by the subject of the origins of Great Zimbabwe never cease to amaze me. A white reader of an earlier manuscript in this series wrote on a draft "The Shona did not build Zimbabwe Ruins !!". I quote here the relevant part of my reply to his comment:

"Now let me try to deal with your assertion that the Shona did not build Great Zimbabwe. It is a statement made by a few white visitors to Great Zimbabwe and it is one which saddens me, particulary in your case coming from a resident white.

"In this case, there is a mountain of evidence which proves your

The Rhodesians sought to prove Great Zimbabwe was not of African origin with material such as this postcard which transposes the Queen of Sheba on the Conical Tower and places a question mark above the Zimbabwe Bird.

7

contention is wrong and ... it is evidence which is in the public domain here in Zimbabwe.

"As a starting point, I commend to you Peter Garlake's book, *Great Zimbabwe*, published by Thames and Hudson in 1973. This has a general editor's preface by one of this century's most distinguished scholars and archaeologists, the late Sir Mortimer Wheeler.

"The book's author, Peter Garlake, is a noted expert on archaeology, architecture, and rock art. From 1964 to 1970, when he was collecting materials for his book, he was the Rhodesian Senior Inspector of Monuments.

"You will find in this book that the British Royal Geographical Society and the British Association for the Advancement of Science both sponsored missions in 1905 and 1929 to ascertain the factual origins of Great Zimbabwe. Their reports, and subsequent radiocarbon dating, show unequivocally that Great Zimbabwe was built by the Shona.

"Wheeler, in his preface, says: 'Alas, tendentious analogies in this vagabond spirit are yet by no means dead' in reference to those who still believe, or would have one believe, that almost anyone but the Shona built Great Zimbabwe. I share his sorrow.

"In his 1905 mission, which included seven excavations, David Randall-MacIver concluded that the Ruins were unmistakably African. Dr Gertrude Caton-Thompson, equipped with advanced technology, followed in 1929 tasked with checking Randall-MacIver's findings.

"Her 1931 report, *The Zimbabwe Culture*, tallies almost entirely with the earlier report of Randall-MacIver. Both of these noted archaeologists, incidentally, were outstanding Middle East scholars, but neither subscribed to the King Solomon, Queen of Sheba, or any other non-African argument, dismissing such as founded in bigotry.

"Radiocarbon dating, which entered the archaeological field of chronology after 1949, has supported the findings of Randall-MacIver and Caton-Thompson".

In conclusion, my letter adds: "I trust it is not a forlorn hope that opinions will be rectified in the future for the facts contained above do not come from 'our government' [meaning black] but Rhodesian sources [meaning white], scientific methods and internationally renowned archaeologists".

There was no written reply to that letter, only a gruff "it doesn't matter" conversation terminator.

Great Zimbabwe, from the time of Cecil Rhodes, has been a political weapon in the settlers' arsenal and it is a weapon they continue to use even though they have lost political power.

The Conical Tower framed by two *muchechete* trees.

Beyond the question of Great Zimbabwe there are many other important ancient historical sites in the country. Among them is the Altar Site outside Mutare where the most important figurines found in this country were unearthed in 1905. Today they are in the vaults of the British Museum, with plaster casts in the vaults of the Mutare Museum. And the site is a rubbish dump.

At Bumbusi Ruins in Hwange there are the remains of a 150-year-old smelting furnace and the walls of another *zimbabwe*. Few tour operators have ever been to the site and it is not on any tourist itinerary. Wild animals and the environment are gradually destroying it. And there are over 200 more *zimbabwes* across the country, many suffering similar neglect.

On the granite faces of caves, largely to the north and east of Harare and in the Matobo Hills near Bulawayo, there is a rich legacy of prehistoric

9

rock art left by the Khoisan. Yet the tour operators and the Zimbabwe government almost entirely ignore it, and they totally ignored an excellent book on the subject by Peter Garlake.

Zimbabwe is not alone in Africa in largely ignoring and failing to promote its rich history. But as the country's name derives not from just Great Zimbabwe but from the many *zimbabwes* scattered across the country, one would have hoped, even expected, that the link between history and the present would be strengthened.

On a recent visit to Ghana, I discovered just how much some west African countries are doing to promote their history, albeit on a limited scale at present, emphasising the barbaric slave trade aspects of the colonial era.

This made me wonder what set Ghana and other west African countries apart from east, central and southern Africa. Generally, they have been independent longer, so that confronting their history is less emotive and sensitive. Also, those running tourism at all levels tend to be largely black Africans.

Perhaps even more important, their wildlife is extremely limited, and they do not have Victoria Falls, both of which distract the Zimbabwean operators, limiting their promotional horizons.

This is nowhere shown more classically than in Zimbabwe's current policy regarding the licensing of guides. Those who take out tourists in the national parks are rigorously tested before they are licensed. But where historical monuments are concerned, no such qualification or knowledge is required. The visitor can be told any nonsense, as is frequently the case.

Zimbabwe still has to learn that it has a history to sell and that visitors are becoming increasingly discerning, and are not simply there to be relieved of hard currency. If they are treated as such, the duration of their visits will diminish.

Beyond the question of history being a marketable commodity, there is a further point succinctly enunciated by the late President of Botswana, Sir Seretse Khama:

"...a nation without a past is a lost nation, and a people without a past is a people without a soul."

GEOLOGY

With the exception of the "gold field" to the immediate north of Great Zimbabwe, the geology of the area is unremarkable, forming part of the late Archaean granite complex known as the Zimbabwe batholith.

This rock forms what is known as the Basement, the oldest and bottom strata found in the region. It is 2,500 million to 3,300 million years old. Weathering over tens of millions of years has exposed parts of the Basement. Elsewhere, this rock is overlain by younger strata.

The huge rock outcrops you will see, locally known as *kopjes* (small hills like irregular massive bubbles), were created by molten rock squeezed up from deep in the earth's crust, cystallising below the surface and then being uplifted and eroded.

These batholith outcrops occur over a large area from Lake Mutirikwi (formerly Kyle) close to Great Zimbabwe and stretch some 40 km south on the road to Beit Bridge.

The existence and abundance of exposed batholith in the area of Great Zimbabwe partially explains why the city was located where it was centuries ago. Great Zimbabwe was not, as was once speculated, situated where it is because of local gold. Hence, the nearby "gold fields" are deliberately put in quotation marks for they were only marginally mined and contained little gold ore.

Zimbabwe's distinctive balancing rocks.

Vervet monkey at dusk on top of a wall at Great Zimbabwe.

ARCHAEOLOGY AND ROCK ART

Some of our ancestors have left their historical records for us to interpret in the prehistoric rock art to be found near Great Zimbabwe, and in many other places in the country. While they are regarded as members of a pre-literate society, nevertheless their paintings are a written record.

Prehistoric rock art and granite are almost inseperable — the first is not usually found without the other. But it does not follow that wherever there is granite, rock art is still to be found. In some areas, such as Bvumba in the Eastern Highlands, there is ample granite, but the conditions are too wet for rock art to have survived.

While the concentration of Zimbabwe's rich heritage of prehistoric rock art exists to the north and east of Harare, and in the Matobo hills near Bulawayo, the Great Zimbabwe area is one of the other parts of the country where prehistoric rock art still exists.

The easiest of the Great Zimbabwe rock-art sites to reach is roughly nine km from Great Zimbabwe on the way to the Mutirikwi dam wall, 150 metres from the main road on a signposted path. Small boys will noisily dispute who will guide you — for a fee — tell you what they learned about rock art in school, and offer to guard your car.

The Chamavara Cave, containing the noted Giant Man of Chamavara surrounded by kudu, is 18 km northeast of the dam wall on Murray MacDougal Drive, and then five km east on a signposted turn-off. A vehicle with good clearance is advised.

One visitor to Chamavara wrote that she found the painting of the human and animal figures confusingly dense and hard to understand. That is true, and the visitor really needs an experienced guide to unravel the fading art and graffiti.

Failing that, your best guide to Zimbabwe's rock art is Peter Garlake's book, *The Hunter's Vision: The Prehistoric Art of Zimbabwe*.

The Khoisan (abbreviated to San), often referred to as Bushmen, were, and on the whole remain, misunderstood and reviled. Like the gypsies in Europe, they were persecuted and largely exterminated.

Most of their artistic sites are unrecorded, and as Garlake notes, "Secrecy is their best protection". Some visitors have thrown water and oil on the paintings to bring out the colour to obtain better photographs. In Spain, two rock paintings have been stolen; the thieves used electric saws to cut the paintings out of the rock.

Most of the rock art one sees at Mutirikwi, Chamavara, and thousands of other sites in Zimbabwe, is between 1,500 and 13,000 years old. The artists were the Khoisan people and their surviving, carefully chosen, and preferred "canvasses", protected from the sun and rain, are most commonly found in granite hills, caves and rock overhangs.

The Khoisan, who were hunter-gatherers, used Stone Age technology, and their artistic legacy projects the imperatives and realities of their world, their perceptions and their beliefs through their own eyes.

Their paintings are "dense", a reflection of the density of animals which existed in their days. They are not the sort of great monuments the visitor may be accustomed to, such as buildings and statues. But, taken in tandem with the vast hills which encompass them, they are huge cultural monuments and a written record of the times.

Numerically, the most common portrayal is of the hunter carrying bows and arrows and with an erect penis. The hunters are depicted as young, athletic and heroic, never old, deformed or ill. Hunting prowess and male potency were major social symbols. Animals are more realistically portrayed than humans.

Women appear less frequently in the paintings. They are portrayed as gatherers by their bags and sticks, and are usually in smaller groups, sometimes accompanied by children. They are plumper, breasts protruding, their buttocks and fronts sometimes covered.

The bows and arrows show that the artists and their subjects were Late Stone Age people. The absence of agricultural or pastoral (with the exception of sheep) activity further dates the works to before the advent of those activities. Dancers, trancers, healers and animals are all portrayed, providing further insights into San society.

Some may find the San art "childish" or "primitive". It is not. As an art form it tends to be dominated by outlines, to be rooted in drawing rather than painting. Colours, usually uniform, fill the space between the extremities of the outline. They are simple and vivid images, not primitive doodlings.

Rock painting.

The paint the San used derived from ironstones and iron oxides in the surrounding area. This was then pounded to a fine powder giving shades of red, brown, ochre, and yellow. White pigments were obtained from kaolin or crushed quartz. Thus the colours used were determined by the locally available materials.

Binding agents, such as animal fat or blood, were mixed with the powdered pigments making the paint dense and easily applied on granite. Application was done by the artists' fingers, coarse brush tips, sometimes made from feathers or a stick pounded at one end to form a brush, or finer brushes. And, unlike modern organic-based plant derivatives, the San's paint did not fade as quickly.

On the periphery of many San paintings one will find paintings which appear more "primitive" than the dominant painting. San society believed that everyone, from the master to rank amateur should try their hand, and this peripheral work is thought to be that of students or children.

The legacy of the San, Great Zimbabwe, the writings of post-literate societies like the Arabs, Portuguese and settler visitors, collectively provide a bridge spanning several centuries to the more distant past.

Our human origins date back some 5 million years to Australopithecus afarensis (Southern ape), through Homo erectus some 1.5 million years ago, and the subsequent stages to humans today.

Through these evolutionary stages, our basic tool kits, artefacts and skills improved, and by the Early Iron Age, around the third century AD, this development was evident throughout eastern and southern Africa. In the area of Great Zimbabwe, the culture became known as the Gokomere Tradition.

These Early Iron Age communities lived in wattle and *daga* (mud) huts not dissimilar to those occupied by some rural people to this day. Pottery and iron smelting were among their most conspicuous skills. They grew millet and sorghum, kept livestock, and were largely self-sufficient, there being little external trade at that stage. Some Late Stone Age skills and habits may have continued into the Iron Age.

New diversities began to appear in the ninth century. As this development accelerated, communities began to fragment, becoming more insular and territorial. This in turn bred ethnic identities, class structures, and perhaps friction. Pottery shapes and decorations proliferated.

This was the background against which Great Zimbabwe began to emerge around 1000 AD, an expression in stone of the birth of a new society.

Decorated 19th century Shona huts with rock kopje behind.

CLIMATE

Guides at Great Zimbabwe used to delight in telling visitors a true story about an African leader who tried to fly there to pay homage as other post-independence state visitors had done before him.

As his helicopter approached from Masvingo, a cloud of mist surrounded the monument in a protective embrace. "The spirits were angry with him. They did not want him to visit," the guides said. His helicopter was forced to turn back.

In fact the cloud of mist which surrounded Great Zimbabwe is a fairly common phenomenon at that time of year known as *guti*, a Shona word for wet mist.

Set on Zimbabwe's central plateau, the Great Zimbabwe and Masvingo area is in the country's climatic middle-range. It is several degrees cooler than Hwange, Victoria Falls and Kariba in the north, and warmer than the Eastern Highlands and Matobo to the west.

As you will find when climbing the Hill Complex in the warmer October/December months, Great Zimbabwe can become quite hot and a cool drink in the cafeteria is exceedingly welcome.

It rains at Great Zimbabwe, as in the rest of the country, from mid-November to mid-March, with unpredictable *guti* before and after the main rains.

Temperatures peak in October/November. Thereafter the weather is mild until April with the main tourist season coming before the next rains. June/July, particularly for locals, can be very cold.

Zimbabwe's national rainfall average of 660 mm (just over 26 inches) is slightly below the world land average, and over the past 50 years has been subject to consequential fluctuations with serious droughts. Great Zimbabwe, in a good year, can get around 1,000 mm.

Sunset over Great Zimbabwe.

GREAT ZIMBABWE'S ORIGINS

The historical home of the Shona people lies roughly between the Zambezi River to the north and Limpopo River to the south. Its east and west boundaries were the Indian Ocean and Kalahari desert respectively. Part of this area now encompasses the Republic of Zimbabwe.

Much of present-day Zimbabwe is set atop a plateau at the southern extremity of the Great Rift which runs from the Red Sea through Ethiopia, east and central Africa, and into southern Africa.

Environment

Three distinct altitudes, with their attendant environmental variations, dominate Zimbabwe. The lowveld is between 300 and 900 metres, includes the Zambezi and Limpopo river valleys, and encompasses much of the southeast of the country. This altitude covers 35 per cent of Zimbabwe.

The middleveld, which includes the area around Great Zimbabwe, is 900 to 1,250 metres and incorporates the central part of Zimbabwe, which is a further 40 per cent of the total. Finally, come the eastern highlands with an altitude of 1,250 to 2,500 metres and the highest rainfall.

Mixed woodland and open savanna dominate the country's vegetation with nutritious "sweet veldt" grass stretching from the south to southwestern extremity of the country. This, as any farmer will tell you, is ideal cattle country as evidenced by the extremely high quality of Zimbabwean beef.

The middleveld falls into Zimbabwe's middle rainfall range with the rains usually coming between November and March.

Thus, the granite provided the building materials for Great Zimbabwe while the vegetation and rainfall dictated its primary economic pursuits — livestock and agriculture. Mining, hunting, trading, manufacturing, fishing and gathering would all have been subsidiary activities in such an environment.

Construction

In the days before transport as we know it, it would have been necessary to minimise the distance between the quarry where the stone was shaped into blocks, and the place to which it must be taken for construction. That would have been a major consideration for the builders of Great Zimbabwe.

The rock outcrops provided an abundance of building material, for conveniently the outcrops exfoliate or "peel", rather like the layers of an onion, with a flattish sheet of rock detaching from the core.

These sheets could be easily trimmed or split into more or less rectangular blocks. This was done at Great Zimbabwe through "firesetting".

Firesetting to make blocks like those used to build Great Zimbabwe is still practised in the area.

Usually "firesetting" is done in the early morning, preferably when there is mist, with water poured onto the fire-heated rock to accelerate breaking, and hammers finally used to shape the blocks.

Before explosives such as dynamite were developed, "firesetting" was common practice until around 1690 in most of Europe and it continued in Germany until a century later. It is a skilled operation, particularly in the cooling process, with an excess of water causing only superficial cracking. In some parts of Africa "firesetting" is still practised, including by Karanga men in the Great Zimbabwe area.

Three possible quarry sites within the immediate area of Great Zimbabwe have been examined — on outcrops at Chivange and Mutuza Hills, and further afield at Heroes' Acre.

The granite found at the first two sites is similar to that used in building the Great Enclosure and is the probable source. The thinner Heroes' Acre granite is believed to have been used in other Great Zimbabwe construction.

So the rock *kopjes* or outcrops literally "peel" into sheets which can be readily divided into more or less rectangular blocks. These blocks were probably manufactured at the base of the rock outcrops and then transported to the building site.

Three methods, singly or together, and depending upon the distance from the quarry site to building, could have been employed. One is the physical transporting of each block by labourers to the building site. But, particularly from Heroes' Acre which is 1.6 km away, this would have been exhausting and time-consuming.

Stone types

In 1961, the walls were classified into four categories and these are still used today:

Class P: uneven courses of varied sized blocks and wavy surfaces between adjacent courses;

Class PQ: intermediate between P and Q;

Class Q: equal sized blocks which form a very regular pattern with the blocks coursed in horizontal layers;

Class R: irregular blocks piled in chaotic style with no evident courses.

The first three classes represent a development sequence with P being the earliest and Q the last. Class R appears to have been used for boundary walls and core filling, rather than for residences.

PQ style construction.

Other methods could have been pulleys, or sledges drawn by people or oxen. The most likely, however, from the closest sites, was probably passing the blocks from hand-to-hand from the quarry to site in much the same way bricks are conveyed to bricklayers to this day.

Not all the blocks fashioned at the quarries would have been of acceptable size as facing blocks. The "rejects" were used in the core of the walls and in places of poorer quality construction.

One must always remember that Great Zimbabwe was built over a period of 300 to 400 years, that in all probability the building was a symbol of the ruler's position in society, and that society then was heavily class-structured.

The protracted period of construction explains the very considerable variation in the walls of Great Zimbabwe. Building skills were developing throughout construction. Some of the structures were for the middle and lower classes, much less grand than those for the king and his entourage.

By simply looking at the various structures, the visitor will observe the progression in the development skills of the masons. The Conical

Chevron pattern at Great Zimbabwe.

Tower and the outer wall of the Great Enclosure in that area, represent the summit of the masons' skills.

Smooth-faced blocks are laid evenly in lines with a looser and more haphazard core which is not keyed to the outer blocks. The faces are battened and the wall tapers upwards.

Towards the top of the eastern side of the outer enclosure chevron decorations are clearly visible. These are in the form of a V, reversed on the lower level, and separated by a single line of blocks. The chevron patterns have narrow blocks of granite at almost 45 degrees and the individual blocks were obviously carefully chosen to achieve the visual effect.

Such chevron patterns are found at other *zimbabwes* in the country, notably at Khami, Dhlo Dhlo and Naletale. At these sites several patterns (dentelle, herringbone, check and cord) are also to be found which reinforces existing archaeological evidence that these were later constructions.

Society
We know that the builders of Great Zimbabwe were Karanga (Shona) and were obviously highly skilled. But beyond that little has been written about the people themselves, their lives, society and economy.

The word Shona is thought to have been used first in the 19th century by white settlers and the Ndebele in South Africa to refer to those who inhabited the area north of the Limpopo River. In all Portuguese records these same people were previously collectively referred to as Karanga.

Thus, the historical evidence appears to indicate that all the Shona once referred to themselves as Karanga and that the word Shona is of foreign origin.

However, the word Shona is now deeply rooted in the society with consequent geo-political divisions and sub-divisions fueling inter-regional tensions. Today the Karanga home area is in the Masvingo and Midlands (including Gweru) area, the Manyika live in the eastern highlands, and the third main Shona grouping, the Zezuru, occupy the Masonaland provinces of the north including Harare.

The Shona, a patrilineal Bantu-speaking people, occupied Zimbabwe in the Late Iron Age (around 1000 AD). They entered the area either from southern Zaire or the Great Lakes area of east Africa.

An early iron hoe head.

They were a cattle-keeping and iron-using agricultural community and in Zimbabwe they encountered what archaeologists refer to as the Gokomere group. This latter group was also an iron-using agricultural community but they apparantly possessed fewer cattle. Their ancestry was probably common and both are believed to have been Bantu-speaking.

Shona society, then and now, is structured in four tiers. At the base is the *imba* or family, headed by the male head of the family. Next comes the *musha* or village, which is headed by the *samusha* or *mwenewomusha*.

Third in the structure comes the *dunhu*, which is a group of villages headed by the *sadunhu*, a sub-chief. Above this is the *nyika* which is headed by the chief or *madzishe* who some also refer to as a *mambo* or king. Some of the *madzishe* built stone structures for themselves and preferred to be called *madzimbabwe*, simply he who dwells in a *zimbabwe*. But this title was reserved for the top level of leadership — the emperors or kings.

The kingdoms and empires were also known as *nyika*. Those such as Munhumatapa and Rozvi regarded themselves as the only true kings and emperors, the *madzimambo*.

At each level, from the family to the ultimate *nyika*, there was a *dare* or council which resolved disputes and meted out punishments. Lower courts could impose minimal sentences while chiefs had legislative as well as judicial powers and derived an income from judicial fees and tribute. A chief did not have a standing army but was able to mobilize his male subjects if the need arose.

Size of chiefdoms (*nyika*) varied from around 30-90 km in length and width, and had well-defined boundaries. The population varied according to size and ecological capacity of the land, but most chiefdoms probably numbered tens of thousands.

The *imba* was the smallest social and production unit. Each member of the family had their own distinct garden with the largest belonging to the head of the household. He grew millet, rice, beans and, after the 16th century, maize. The women grew groundnuts, peanuts, pumpkins, beans, cucumbers and yams.

Much has been written about the men being lazy and the women doing all the work. But work was apportioned and considerable time had to be devoted to attending festivals or work parties to ensure that neighbours helped in harvesting crops.

One of Zimbabwe's most outstanding historians, Dr Stan Mudenge, in his book *A Political History of Munhumatapa c. 1400-1902*, noted that kinship was the most important aspect of village life, "an all-embracing ideology". To a large extent this remains the case, helping to explain many current political and economic actions.

At the *imba* or family unit the residents would naturally be related. At the *musha* or village level some outsiders *(vatorwa)* begin to enter the scene, always with the specific permission of the *samusha*.

Gradually, as one moves up the scale and communities become larger, the blood line thins, with more *vatorwa* being embraced by the extended family, through marriage (frequently used to forge kinship relations), acceptance or conquest.

Young boy herding cattle.

The *musha,* or village, remains the basic economic unit of production. And within this unit tasks were assigned.

Hunting, tending cattle and clearing new ground were male responsibilities. Women were responsible for domestic tasks such as cleaning and cooking, brewing beer, making earthenware utensils, weeding gardens, pounding grain and gathering.

Judged by today's standards Shona society is regarded as "sexist" with men retaining control of major decision-making and economic/trading areas, restricting women to a subservient role, and maintaining the *dare* or council as a male preserve.

In this, Shona society has many parallels with other cultures and like them must confront the past to forge the future with all the attendant unknowns. Conservatives cling to the past, values change and generation gaps emerge. It is an evolutionary process, too fast for some, too slow for others.

One major change which has occurred affects the Shona week. The Mutapa and his people divided the month into three ten-day weeks with holidays *(zvisi)* on the fourth and seventh days of each week. The month began with the arrival of the new moon and concluded at the end of each 30-day lunar cycle.

A Karanga spirit medium.

Ancestor veneration and spirit possession were other vital components of society in which institutional conservatism flows upwards from the grassroots to the centre with the former dictating much of the pace of change.

Great Zimbabwe was built by the Karanga (Shona) people to dominate the cattle-grazing areas of the country as well as to exact tribute *(mupeto)* from the gold-mines.

In essence, as Mudenge puts it, the Shona people were "masters of the peaceful arts" depending for their wealth on agriculture, mining, trading and building, while creating political and religious institutions.

Economy

The pastoral environment and local availability of stone dictated where Great Zimbabwe was built. However, a map identifying known prehistoric gold and copper mines, and the juxtaposition of *zimbabwes* to them, particularly those which were decorated, proposes subsidiary reasons.

Very few of the earliest known mines are without adjacent *zimbabwes*. Most of those close to the mines (and the distance is usually around one kilometre) are undecorated, while the decorated *zimbabwes*, like Great Zimbabwe itself, tend to be further removed.

This suggests that the mines were owned, controlled, and their trade directed by the head of each *zimbabwe*.

When one looks at the mines/*zimbabwes* distribution map, one immediately notes the discrepancy in distance from the mines between decorated and undecorated *zimbabwes*.

Such a stratified society has a parallel in contemporary Zimbabwe and all other communities. The upper class, defined by money, status, or both, aspires to the more prestigious northern suburbs of Harare. The middle class is to be found in the avenues and less expensive suburbs, and the working class in the townships.

Given what we know about the nature of society, then and now, it is not surprising that the richest members of the society lived some distance from the source of their wealth, much as is the case today with the rulers in urban capitals living some distance from the rural areas.

Many parallels can be found with this structure in the societies of pre-Industrial Revolution feudal Europe. The ruler or squire lived in the castle or manor, usually in the country surrounded by good agricultural land and cattle. There they would be distanced from their mines or industries. That would be Great Zimbabwe and the decorated *zimbabwes*.

That ruler or squire had bailiffs and tenant farmers, like those who ran Great Zimbabwe and occupied the other *zimbabwes*. And at the bottom of the social ladder came the labourers. All paid tribute (tax) to the ruler through their labour and their production.

And why would the rulers of Great Zimbabwe then not have controlled their state (which was five times the size of England) through a sort of "extended family": through direct relatives of the leader, through relatives by marriage, and through subjects owing allegiance?

Great Zimbabwe was the furthest removed decorated *zimbabwe* from the mines. It was the seat of the region's culture which stretched into today's eastern Botswana to the west, as far east as contemporary Mozambique's Indian Ocean coastline, and well into South Africa.

Historians, archaeologists and geologists agree that Great Zimbabwe was removed from the mining complexes, straddling an area which was climatically good for human habitation and where the grasslands provided plentiful year-round grazing for cattle.

Bones from cattle found in domestic rubbish mounds indicate that the elite of the society was highly dependent upon beef. Most of the bones are of younger animals which further indicates that the breeding herds, as the providers of the main food, were kept further away and protected. The younger meat, it is speculated, was provided for the king by his subjects as a tribute or tax.

The importance of cattle in Shona society cannot be over-emphasised. Apart from providing food, cattle are used for *lobola* (the bride price), slaughtered after burials (*kurova guva,* which is similar to a wake) and following victories. They are used for patronage, and above all to measure individuals' wealth and thereby their status in society. They are in reality mobile bank accounts.

Carver at work.

Cereal production existed, mainly for *sadza* (a thick, porridge-like staple eaten with beef or vegetable stew locally known as relish) and beer. There is evidence that some artefacts were also made at Great Zimbabwe; a coppersmith's forge and tools having been found in the Great Enclosure. Affiliated to this, crucibles, ingots, wire used for making bracelets and anklets, and moulds have been found. There was also a textile industry, jewellery-making from gold, pottery-making and soapstone-sculpting.

While the Zimbabwe Birds are the most famous artefacts recovered they are by no means the only artefacts to have been found.

Six geometrically decorated and complete soapstone platters, and many fragments of platters, have been found, as have many soapstone figurines.

The most important finds, other than the Zimbabwe Birds, were made in the Valley Complex. These included 100 kg of iron hoes, axes, chisels, an iron gong, and strikers. Over 20 kg of twisted iron wire, ready to turn into bangles, and a stone mould used for casting copper ingots, were also among the 1902 finds.

The imported items include many thousands of tiny coloured glass beads, probably made in India. Also found were 13th century glazed Chinese celadon dishes in delicate hues, a 14th century Persian bowl, Far Eastern glazed stoneware, copper jewellery, gold, elephant and warthog tusks.

The site of these finds is known today as the Royal Treasury. Some of the treasure would have been paid to the king by way of tribute, other items; such as those originating in China and India, would have been traded with the Arab and Asian traders operating on the east African coast.

Some of these items were deposited in the museum where the Zimbabwe Birds are housed. Unfortunately however, some of the items deposited have been stolen by latter-day treasure seekers.

Thus many of the more practical, as well as the more esoteric crafts were practised at Great Zimbabwe. Its ruler controlled a vast swathe of territory, including the area of mining activity, and his kingdom produced the beef (and milk) upon which the elite depended as their main source of protein.

It was a highly integrated economy with the raw materials for the crafts at Great Zimbabwe coming from other parts of the kingdom: gold from all over present-day Zimbabwe; copper from the mines, probably in the extreme north of Mashonaland and south of the Limpopo River around Messina in South Africa; stone for the carvers from at least 25 km away.

Their society, politically and environmentally changed little until the 19th century Nguni invasions from South Africa, and the Indian Ocean trading posts such as Kilwa and Malindi evolved because of the trading potential of the Munhumatapa Empire.

Thus, it is wrong to over-emphasise the importance of Portuguese-Mutapa relations because of the extensive Portuguese written records.

And equally it is wrong to believe that a trading post is established in an area without potential customers. The Munhumatapa Empire would have been the *raison d'etre* for Arab, Asian and Portuguese activity.

Controlling and maintaining this economic and political State would have required great organisation and military muscle.

Construction at Great Zimbabwe began around 1100 AD. It was in decline leading to abandonment between 1450 and 1500 AD. Linguists say that it was a pre-literate society, and thus has left no written records to answer the many questions which perplex historians, only oral history passed down from generation to generation.

In the early 17th century a Portuguese priest, Father João dos Santos, wrote of the Karanga: "They can neither read nor write, and have no books, and all ancient history and other things which they know they learn by tradition from their ancestors."

However, and this is a very important point, those non-Shona societies which some claim built Great Zimbabwe were literate. Yet they left no written record suggesting they built Great Zimbabwe.

Decline
The earliest known written reference to Zunbanhy (thought to have been Zimbabwe), comes in 1506 in a letter to the King of Portugal (see next section). By then Great Zimbabwe was in decline and the reasons for this, and its abandonment, fall into the realm of speculation.

What we do know is that Great Zimbabwe had become home to between 10,000 and 18,000 people (depending upon whose figures you accept). It was the largest stone structure and the largest city in sub-Saharan Africa. Beyond that, it was the centre of a sprawling cultural tradition.

One can easily imagine the social needs of such a population and the pressures it created. The demand for beef would have been increasing. So would the demand for pasture. Massive deforestation would have been inevitable as people cut down trees to cook their food. That in turn would have affected rainfall patterns.

While not proposing the ecological argument as a single explanation for the decline and fall of Great Zimbabwe, the monument does leave us one most important lesson regarding environmental preservation.

In Zimbabwe today, deforestation occurs for four main reasons. People cut trees to build houses, stockade their animals, clear land to grow crops, and cook their food. The use of stone at Great Zimbabwe would have removed two reasons for felling trees, ie houses and animals.

For many years historians and archaeologists sought a single reason for the decline and final abandonment of Great Zimbabwe.

Today, a more rational interpretation rejects the mono-causal approach, instead accepting that there was probably a sequence of interwoven factors of which environmental degradation was an important one.

Overgrown area around the Conical Tower before clearance from the late 19th century.

COLONIAL HISTORY

It is necessary to separate what we actually know about Great Zimbabwe from the plethora of academic speculation and politically motivated myth.

Portuguese

The first known written reference to the Mutapa State comes in a letter in 1506 from Diogo de Alcacova to the King of Portugal. It refers to "Zunbanhy" saying that the "houses of the king [Munhumutapa] ... were of stone and clay, very large and on one level". In 1511, a Portuguese explorer, Antonio Fernandes, added the important footnote that the stones were held together without mortar.

An aloe offsets a wall laid without mortar.

There is a dispute over these two references. It is argued that they did not refer to Great Zimbabwe but to the capital of the Mutapa state further north.

However, insofar as the next reference is concerned, scholars agree this was definitely to Great Zimbabwe.

In 1552, a Portuguese historian, João de Barros, who had not visited Great Zimbabwe, referred to it in *Da Asia*, the first volume of the history of Portuguese conquests. His account is secondhand and vague in places. But it is an invaluable record which historians routinely quote from.

De Barros admitted that it was not known who built the "edifice", which he describes as the court of Benomotapa [Munhumutapa]. The Moorish traders who were de Barros' source said it was very ancient, built to keep possession of the mines.

De Barros speculates that Great Zimbabwe was built by "some prince" (a vassal of Munhumutapa) who had possession of the mines. He makes reference to the similarity between Great Zimbabwe and "...the land of Prester John, at a place called Acaxumo, which was a municipal city of the Queen of Sheba".

This is the first written reference to the Queen of Sheba, the speculation being subsequently transformed into myth, and then "fact", in an attempt to justify occupation of the land.

In the middle of the mines, de Barros wrote, "...there is a square fortress, masonry within and without, built of stones of marvellous size, and there appears to be no mortar joining them.

"The wall is more than twenty-five spans [a span is nine inches] in width, and the height is not so great considering its width. Above the door of this edifice is an inscription, which some Moorish merchants, learned men, who went thither, could not read, neither could they tell what the character might be."

A further reference to the Queen of Sheba, although this time in reference to another *zimbabwe* further north, is made in 1609 by Joao dos Santos, a Portuguese missionary who had worked at the Mutapa's court from 1586 to 1595. And for good measure King Solomon is now added.

In 1616, in a subsequent volume of *Da Asia*, dos Santos' successor Diogo de Couto referred again to the Queen of Sheba obtaining her gold from the Great Zimbabwe area. Such trade was possible, even probable. De Couto does not suggest the Queen of Sheba built Great Zimbabwe.

Thus several centuries before the Rhodesian settlers arrived, Portuguese sources had speculated, that Great Zimbabwe had foreign trading links, although they stopped well short of saying it was foreign built. Their speculation would appear to have been motivated by the notion that the vast and unknown African interior contained an abundance of wealth.

A land of such abundant riches became part of the folklore of Europe to be repeated — and believed — in one country after another. Such would have been the childhood fables and comics upon which Cecil Rhodes was nurtured.

German

Another person who believed such stories was a German missionary in the eastern Transvaal, the Reverend Alex Merensky. In 1868, he met a young German geologist, Carl Mauch, who was also captivated by the stories. In May 1871, Mauch embarked on a journey north to seek "the most valuable and important and hitherto most mysterious part of Africa ... the old Monomatapa [sic] or Ophir".

Carl Mauch, the first foreigner to publicise Great Zimbabwe in Europe.

Near Great Zimbabwe, he met Adam Render, an American of German origin, who had deserted his ship and made his home in the Karanga area where he married Chief Pika's daughter. Mauch, who referred to Render as "a white kaffir" because he now had two African wives, provides the first detailed written description of Great Zimbabwe:

"The ruins may be divided into two parts: the one upon a granite rocky eminence of 400 feet in height, the other upon a somewhat elevated terrace. The two are separated by a gentle valley, their distance apart being about 300 yards. The rocky bluff consists of an elongated mass of granite, rounded in form, upon which stands a second block, and upon this again fragments smaller, but still many tons in weight, with fissures, chasms and cavities.

"The western side of the mountain is covered from top to bottom by the ruins. As they are for the most part fallen in and covered with rubbish, it is at present impossible to determine the purpose the buildings were intended to serve; the most probable is that it was a fortress in those times, and this the many passages — now, however, walled up — and the circular or zigzag plan of the walls would also indicate.

"All the walls, without exception, are built without mortar, of hewn granite, more or less about the size of our bricks... Best preserved of all is the outer wall of an erection of rounded form, situated in the plain, and about 150 yards in diameter. It is at a distance of about 600 yards from the mountain, and was probably connected with it by means of great outworks, as appears to be indicated by the mounds of rubbish remaining...

Evening shadows on the Great Enclosure wall.

"Inside, everything excepting a tower nearly 30 feet in height, and in perfect preservation, is fallen to ruins, but this, at least, can be made out; that the narrow passageways are disposed in the form of a labyrinth."

Mauch's eyewitness description of Great Zimbabwe at that point is speculative on one point only, its purpose — a fortress. Historians now generally agree that its purpose was to symbolise the power and prestige of the ruling class. Otherwise it is a factual account of how he saw the ruins and to a large extent how we still see them, today. Importantly, Mauch indicates there were then mounds of rubbish left by earlier occupants, and that they were overgrown.

Other aspects of Mauch's three visits to Great Zimbabwe, however, are less accurate. A piece of wood he cut from the collapsed lintel of one doorway smelt like cedar, conclusive proof, he felt, that it had been brought by the Phoenicians. It has subsequently been proved that the wood was *tambooti*, a local African hardwood.

Mauch's description, and erroneous interpretations of the origins of Great Zimbabwe, were widely published and accepted in Germany and elsewhere. This ensured that the stories emanating from the Moors and passed on by the Portuguese were now, with major political distortions, about to enter Rhodesian history.

British
On one point, historians and archaeologists are in agreement: Willi Posselt, Richard Hall, and other early excavators at Great Zimbabwe were treasure seekers who had no knowledge of, or regard for, the scientific evidence they were destroying.

Such unanimity suggests the highly unlikely prognosis that had those early treasure seekers not destroyed the evidence they did, then the historians and archaeologists would have been able to agree, and accurately interpret Great Zimbabwe for us.

While not excusing the destruction wrought by those early white visitors, their behaviour was perfectly understandable when set against the imperatives of the time, and the reason why they were at Great Zimbabwe in the first place.

Gold and diamonds had been found in huge quantities in South Africa. The belief was — and this was re-emphasised by early explorers, hunters and missionaries — that a veritable El Dorado or second Witwatersrand lay across the Limpopo River.

It was this erroneous belief that led to the granting of a Royal Charter, the formation of the British South Africa Company (BSAC), and the Pioneer Column's invasion of Mashonaland and later Matabeleland.

Initially, the settlers had no interest in the land — for science or agriculture — as evidenced by their obtaining only mining concessions from local rulers.

In 1889, Willi Posselt visited Great Zimbabwe from South Africa during a trading and hunting expedition. A local guide had told him of stone images representing a King and Queen whom Posselt immediately assumed were King Solomon and the Queen of Sheba.

After contacting the local chief, whose name Posselt spells as Umgabe (Mugabe, not related to Zimbabwe's President), Posselt was provided with a guide to take him to the ruins.

On 14 August 1889, he saw Great Zimbabwe. He records he was told that years earlier the site had been occupied by the Barozwi (Rozvi), that they had offered periodic sacrifices, and that the site was still regarded as sacred by the local people.

Having failed to find the stone images he described as "King Solomon and the Queen of Sheba", nor any human remains or implements, Posselt wrote, "my hope of discovering some treasure was not rewarded with success."

Posselt returned to Great Zimbabwe on the same journey and was taken to the Hill Complex. There, he saw four soapstone Zimbabwe Birds facing east.

"Each one, including its plinth, had been hewn out of a solid block of stone and measured four feet six inches in height; and each was set firmly into the ground. There was also a stone shaped like a mill-stone and about eighteen inches in diameter, with a number of figures carved on the border. Soapstone is a sort of schist [a serpentine or soft, talc-rich metamorphic rock], and lends itself easily to the tool of the sculptor. It is also very durable.

"I selected the best specimen of the four bird stones, the beaks of the remainder being damaged, and decided to dig it out. But while doing so, Andizibi [This was Haruzivishe, a relative of Chief Mugabe who lived on the Hill Complex] and his followers became very excited and rushed around with their guns and assegais. I fully expected them to attack us. However, I went on with my work, but told Klass [a Sotho member of the party], who had loaded two rifles, to shoot the first man he saw aiming at either of us."

The Zimbabwe Bird, with base cut off, which Posselt sold to Rhodes.

Posselt says he assured "Andizibi" that he would buy the stones and the next day paid for them "with some blankets and other articles."

"I received the one stone bird and the perforated stone. The former was too heavy to be carried and I was therefore obliged to cut off the pedestal. I stored the remaining stones in a secure place, it being my intention to return at a future date and secure them from the natives."

The vandalisation of Great Zimbabwe had begun.

Posselt retraced his route to South Africa where "A report got about that we had visited King Solomon's Temple and had brought some wonderful stones." This culminated in Rhodes buying the first soapstone bird known to have been taken from Great Zimbabwe.

Rhodesia
Rhodes and Posselt were to meet for the first time in 1896 in Southern Rhodesia during the Anglo-Ndebele War. Posselt records that Rhodes told him: "Often in Cape Town when I speak to the people about the Hinterland, some of them take no notice; others have no faith in that wild country. But then I take that stone bird you found in the Zimbabwe Ruins; I place it on the table, and tell them that where this bird came from there must be something else."

Brought up on the stories of the fabulous wealth of the African interior, owner of the first soapstone bird taken from Great Zimbabwe, and equipped with a Royal Charter supporting his commercial expansionist plans, Rhodes' "Pioneer Column" in 1890 invaded and captured Mashonaland — in the name of Britain.

Rhodes Pioneers hoist the British flag.

Rhodes now needed "scientific" proof to justify his invasion, which in his view was to show that colonialism was part and parcel of returning the country from "barbaric" hands to the former "civilisation" and majesty he imagined.

In 1891, only a year after the conquest of Mashonaland, Rhodes, with the help of the Royal Geographical Society and the British Association for the Advancement of Science, sponsored a mission by J. Theodore Bent to investigate the origins of Great Zimbabwe.

Bent had travelled in the eastern Mediterranean and Persian Gulf seeking the origins of the Phoenicians. Given the prevailing belief about the origins of Great Zimbabwe, he was an ideal candidate even if he lacked any scientific skills.

Significantly however, upon seeing Great Zimbabwe, Bent observed: "Now of course it is a great temptation to talk of Phoenician ruins when there is anything like gold to be found in connection with them, but from my own personal experience of Phoenician ruins I cannot say that [Great Zimbabwe] bears the slightest resemblance whatsoever."

Generally, what Bent unearthed during his two months of excavations pointed to the ruins being a "native", meaning local, antiquity. Work at the Great Enclosure was abandoned after only two weeks in favour of the Hill Complex in the hope that the latter site would "... be free of Kaffir desecration," Bent wrote. But that was not to be.

Bent.

Most of the finds were similar to those being used by the Karanga in the area. The soapstone birds and a few other items offered the main hope of distancing Great Zimbabwe from the local people, and through a process of subjective selection of artefacts, Bent sought to substantiate the myths surrounding Great Zimbabwe.

He concluded that: "The ruins and the things in them are not in any way connected with any known African race," and therefore the builders of Great Zimbabwe probably came from the Arabian peninsula. Despite Bent's findings being riddled with obvious contradictions, they helped to justify Rhodes' invasion in the eyes of a less than questioning public 10,000 miles away in Europe.

In September 1895, the BSAC (meaning Rhodes), after he had acquired over 200 ounces of necklaces and beads found on skeletons at another *zimbabwe*, granted exclusive rights to the Rhodesia Ancient Ruins Company "to explore and work for treasure" at several specified ruins in Matabeleland. The BSAC was to receive 20 per cent of the finds, Rhodes would have the first option to purchase all discoveries, and at his express wish, Great Zimbabwe was excluded from the agreement.

The Rhodesia Ancient Ruins Company, while recovering little of monetary value to themselves or Rhodes, were wreaking terrible destruction on the country's ancient monuments. A local freelance journalist, Richard Hall, then tried in 1902 to give respectability to the company in his book, *The Ancient Ruins of Rhodesia.*

While the book itself was extremely poor, it brought a turning point in Hall's life. In financial difficulties, Hall had been sent back to Britain by the BSAC in 1900. A year later, in similar difficulties, Hall was employed by Rhodes, becoming the first "curator" of Great Zimbabwe.

Rhodes employed Hall in the BSAC, despite the protests of his directors and colleagues, but initially only gave him a six-month contract at Great Zimbabwe. His short-term contract can be interpreted in several ways.

One would be that Rhodes limited it because of his colleagues' objections.

The second is that Rhodes struck a deal with Hall, giving the latter adequate time to travel to and from Cape Town, recover the three cached birds, and deliver them to Rhodes.

Rhodes, however, died on 26 March 1902, and his mentor's death removed any private undertaking Hall may have made.

In the event, Hall greatly overstepped his initial, ill-defined mandate. He began removing trees, creepers, undergrowth, fallen stones and several feet of precious archaeological deposits, to remove "the filth and decadence of the kaffir occupation."

External criticism of Hall's "reckless blundering" and "indescribable" field work,

Hall and the Zimbabwe Bird he found in 1903.

led the BSAC to remove him from the post in early 1904. But by then an incalculable amount of damage had been done.

Zimbabwe

Pressure from more expert circles in Britain, coupled with the BSAC's need to repair its tarnished image, led directly to the British Association for the Advancement of Science, with funding from the Rhodes Trustees, sending a trained archaeologist, Dr David Randall-MacIver, to unravel the myths and facts about Great Zimbabwe.

Randall-MacIver had been a student, and later colleague, of the highly regarded Middle Eastern scholar, Sir Flinders Petrie, who had pioneered a new scientific approach to archaeology in Eygpt. Randall-MacIver was determined to be objective in his work, being aware of, but not bound by, myths created over the previous four centuries.

The finding by Randall-MacIver that Great Zimbabwe had been constructed by Africans infuriated the white settlers and their conservative supporters overseas. Their view, held until this day, was that locals who "knew the natives" were superior in their judgements to scientific experts from overseas.

The hornet's nest released by Randall-MacIver's findings remained until 1929. That year, once again, the Rhodes Trustees and British Association for the Advancement of Science collaborated in yet another attempt to investigate the origins of Great Zimbabwe.

This time they chose Dr Gertrude Caton-Thompson, another highly qualified archaeologist who had worked in Eygpt, to find definitively on Randall-MacIver's verdict and Hall's response.

Her report was even more devastating than Randall-MacIver's. She concurred with him, saying there was not a single scrap of evidence from her excavations and finds which was "...not in accordance with the claim of Bantu origin and medieval date".

Theoretically, Caton-Thompson's report reinforcing Randall-MacIver's findings, should have finalised the matter. But now new forces began to dictate the terms of the debate.

Black nationalists after the Second World War increasingly associated their struggle against settler rule with the word Zimbabwe. Their liberation movements, which were to triumph at the end of the 1970s, were known as the Zimbabwe African National Union (ZANU) and Zimbabwe African People's Union (ZAPU).

ZANU and ZAPU were banned for their political activity by the settler goverment which continued to refuse to accept the scientific findings of Randall-MacIver and Caton-Thompson. In 1970 the settlers went a step further, formally ordering that no official publication could state unequivocally that Great Zimbabwe had been created by Africans.

In April 1980, the Republic of Zimbabwe was born. It had been a tortuous journey during which myths had evolved, Mashonaland and later Matabeleland had been invaded, evidence at Great Zimbabwe had been destroyed, racial barriers erected, and a war fought.

THREE WALKS AROUND GREAT ZIMBABWE

For the visitor's benefit, the tour of Great Zimbabwe can be divided into three walks starting from the cafeteria and craft shop at the foot of the Hill Complex.

The first is to the Hill Complex, up via the ancient path and down by the modern path. Next comes the Valley Enclosure and, finally, the Great Enclosure, ending at the museum where the Zimbabwe Birds are kept. The walks can be done in any order.

It is not desirable, if one is to absorb the surroundings, to try to do the three walks in one session. The climb to the Hill Complex is quite steep, and particularly in the hotter months it is advisable to do this early in the day when it is cooler. The Valley Complex also involves some slopes, albeit less steep, while the Great Enclosure is generally flat.

The Hill Complex and the weathered granite of the *kopje* from the Great Enclosure.

Hill Complex

Visitors, no doubt more familiar with Greek ruins, refer to the Hill Complex as the Acropolis. While for some that name has stuck, it is inappropriate as this is an African and not a Greek monument.

The hill was inhabited by Stone Age hunter-gatherers, as well as early and late Iron Age people, before Great Zimbabwe was built. It rises 80 metres above the valley floor and its northern face is bare granite, some 30 metres in height and 100 metres in length. Sections of the granite show exfoliation, and in some places it is stained black and grey most of the year, mud-streaked during the rains.

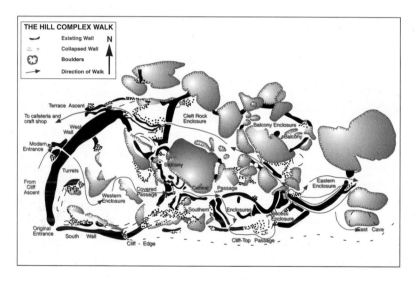

There are at least three ways in which the Hill Complex is accessed. One, which is rarely used, is the Terrace Ascent (or Watergate Path) from the north or main road. A fourth access, possibly older than any of the others, may have been discovered in early 1997. It is still to be explored by archaeologists.

The heavily walled ancient path, or Cliff Ascent as some call it, is better confronted going up than down because it is slippery during the rains, steep, and both the steps and width of the path are very narrow in places. It is also the quickest way to the top, best climbed when you are fresh.

You begin through a stone gateway adjoining the 900-metre-long inner perimeter wall which has largely collapsed. This gateway is a reconstruction which imitates earlier structures with rounded entrances, buttresses and towers. Just off the path to the right is a large pit from which *daga* (mud) was extracted and carried up the hill to build huts.

At the top of the ancient path you will first encounter the West Wall of the Western or Royal Enclosure. This is a most impressive structure, the largest wall on the Hill Complex, standing eight metres high and five metres wide at the top.

West Wall and pillars/turrets.

On top of the wall are traces of turrets and pillars which you can see from a considerable distance, from the Great Enclosure and the main road below. Once, it is believed, these pillars and turrets existed every two metres. Today, only two pillars and four turrets remain.

All accesses to the Hill Complex meet at the West Wall which the visitor passes through via a modern entrance into the Western Enclosure. This entrance collapsed because the lintels of local hardwood had outlived their life span and decayed, and stone lintels were incorrectly used to replace them.

The wall itself is ancient, constructed in uneven P style. But the visitor will note variations in the coursed stonework where incorrect restoration occurred in the 1920s which borrowed from the later Q style.

The Hill Complex was the first part of Great Zimbabwe to be built and the remaining original stonework reflects this greater antiquity, with masonry becoming more refined elsewhere at Great Zimbabwe as the builders' skills developed.

Through the modern entrance the visitor enters the Royal Enclosure which was the main living area for successive kings for around 300 years. This is confirmed by the discovery at the site of several royal items including a serrated bronze spear, a crescent-shaped battle axe, gongs, soapstone bowls and gold, as well as by oral tradition.

The only remaining original doorway at Great Zimbabwe leading from the Western Enclosure of the Hill Complex.

Excavations have shown that as one hut decayed, so another was built on the same foundations. Despite much of the archaeological evidence having been shovelled over the cliff to clear the site, the sides of irregular pits still reveal this construction progression.

A 1958 excavation of deposits which had not been tampered with, in the northeast of this enclosure, revealed the clearest chronological sequence to date.

There were few stones in the enclosure and in the earliest period in the sequence, huts were built from *daga* before stone was used, showing this is the oldest of Great Zimbabwe's three areas.

As one still finds in the newer Great Enclosure, the Royal Enclosure of the Hill Complex had inner and outer walls, separated by passages.

The South Wall, set on the edge of the granite cliff, offers a spectacular view of the Great Enclosure and Valley Complex below. Sections of the wall have now tumbled down the cliff, and interestingly a modern reconstruction of part of the wall, which attempted to cross a crevice, collapsed during the rains in early 1997, while the original structures remained intact.

A view of the Great Enclosure from the Hill Complex.

The north and east walls incorporate the natural rock formations, building upon and not around them. The lessons of this appear to have reached contemporary architects who used similar methods at Lobo Lodge in Tanzania's Serengeti National Park in the 1960s, and more recently in the construction of the Lodge at the Ancient City near Great Zimbabwe. In both cases nature is harnessed, not ignored or blasted into oblivion.

A walled balcony, now filled in as a safety precaution, stood ten metres above the enclosure. One of the Zimbabwe Birds in the museum was found hidden in boulders near this balcony.

The narrow exit from the Western Enclosure to the east is covered and is the only original entrance left intact at Great Zimbabwe. Through it the visitor enters the walled Central Passage leading to a series of other smaller enclosures.

First come the Southern Enclosures, the Recess Enclosure and the Eastern or Sacred Enclosure. All these, archaeologists believe, were linked, possibly by a cliff-top pathway. Buttresses, built on the natural rocks, make progress from one enclosure to the next slow, and they would have afforded the occupants a measure of protection and privacy.

These enclosures, where most of the Zimbabwe Birds were found, are thought to have been the seat of the medium or mediums who would have been possessed by one of the most important ancestral spirits.

The Eastern Enclosure has been the subject of much speculation and it continues to fascinate. It is set against a cliff amidst the most dramatic boulders.

Above it, with the boulders as a backdrop, were a series of small platforms with steps leading to them from the lower passage. The platforms were decorated with *daga* and on the platforms stood many stone pillars, on top of some of which were Zimbabwe Birds.

Theodore Bent found six Zimbabwe Birds in this enclosure including two miniatures. Three were in the northwest corner, standing together against a fallen boulder. One was in the centre on a circular platform. The other two were on a platform to your right as you enter the enclosure from its eastern entrance.

As you leave the enclosure towards the west, a huge boulder towers over you blocking the view. Its weather-sculpted features bear a remarkable resemblance to a Zimbabwe bird. The forehead is flat, the neck long, the breast of the boulder swells like that of a bird. Could this have been the inspiration for the Zimbabwe Birds and their placement in the Eastern Enclosure, archaeologists ask?

Further on, towards the edge of the cliff, there is a cave in which iron ore can still be found. Some people claim, using a liberal dose of poetic licence, that the acoustics are such that an order shouted here is heard in the valley below.

For Shona traditionalists, the cave remains synonymous with Great Zimbabwe, and they freqently leave materials here of cultural significance such as black cloth, snuff and other gifts.

From the Eastern Enclosure the visitor enters the Balcony Enclosure and Cleft Rock Enclosure through narrow, but tressed passageways between the boulders.

From the Cleft Rock Enclosure the descent to the northern part of the West Wall is fairly steep. In this area there was considerable evidence of early human habitation such as ash, litter and *daga* floors, where once there were huts. This debris of human activity was covered with six metres of rubble and held back by a decorated retaining wall.

This area appears to have been a residential complex where many of those residing on the Hill Complex lived in close proximity to the ruler in the Western or Royal Enclosure.

Descending the Hill Complex on the modern path the visitor will see the Terrace Ascent or Watergate Path on their right. This route is an original one, but today it is overgrown, rough and littered with collapsed walling.

An example of walling blending in with existing granite.

Valley Complex

On my earliest visits to Great Zimbabwe I gave the Valley Complex a miss. That I learned was a mistake, for this area contains an abundance of Great Zimbabwe's history, both ancient and more modern.

At first sight the Valley Complex is confusing and it appears less significant than the Hill Complex and Great Enclosure. Enclosures and walls are on a smaller scale but, nevertheless, they exist, as do other facets of Great Zimbabwe such as turrets, buttresses, platforms, pillars, and the traces of where huts once stood.

Each enclosure or courtyard appears to have once housed a family unit and 42 of these have been counted. They would have been the homes of lesser members of the court, possibly the junior wives of the king, and their attendants.

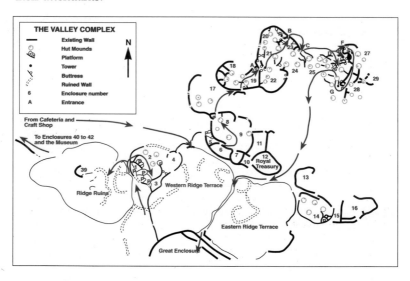

Moving with your back towards the cafeteria and curio shop across an open area, you first encounter the West Ridge Terrace joined to the Great Enclosure to your right by a wall. This discreetly signposted terrace is the largest and best preserved structure in the Valley Complex.

The terrace is entered from a passageway. The entrance is unusually grooved and the wall on the right is particularly impressive. After entering, and to the visitors right, there are high, large platforms,

Part of the Valley Complex.

through which an inner enclosure is reached. Further to your right there are more platforms and several hut mounds.

Unfortunately, much of this area was ransacked in 1892 by the second-in-command of the "Pioneer Column", Major Sir John Willoughby, and a force of labourers tasked with hunting for treasure.

From the Western Ridge Terrace, the visitor arrives at the inappropriately named Renders Ruins, a sprawling, irregular-shaped area. Archaeologically this could have housed some of the most important finds. But, unfortunately, most of the evidence was destroyed by treasure seekers before scientists arrived on the scene.

This enclosure was the Royal Treasury. In it the tribute paid to the king, iron and copper, and imported items such as beads, would have been kept. But the site was looted by Hall in 1902 and only the remnants he discarded, or missed, have found their way to the nearby museum.

The visitor leaves this area through a collapsed doorway and over a raised platform, for the Central Valley, which contained the main population density at Great Zimbabwe.

These ruins have the finest and best coursed brickwork remaining in the valley. Short walls jut out from the surrounding enclosure towards *daga* huts forming inner enclosures and affording a measure of privacy for the residents.

There were six, still discernable, entrances to this area. Following the entrances and routes connecting various enclosures, one has the impression that there was a screening process.

These entrances probably marked the ruler's boundary, with the ordinary people living outside the perimeter wall. At each step along the way the visitor would have to be cleared before proceeding to the next point, rather as security works today. The narrowness of the routes connecting the enclosures (sometimes only wide enough for one person) would have made it fairly easy to protect the inhabitants at the centre of the hive of enclosures.

To the southeast of this area, the visitor arrives at a granite pillar, the only surviving one in the complex. It is here in 1903 that Hall found the Zimbabwe Bird which today appears on coins, the flag, emblems, and a great many other things. It is the best preserved of the Zimbabwe Birds and the only one not found on the Hill Complex.

Next on the visitor's path comes the Eastern Valley. It was in this relatively undisturbed area that Caton-Thompson conducted her careful archaeological excavations in 1929, proving conclusively for those willing to accept the scientific evidence that Great Zimbabwe had been constructed and occupied by the Shona people.

Carbon dating

Radiocarbon dating, a scientific method not developed until 1949, and still being refined, finally laid to rest many of the myths created about Great Zimbabwe.

As a result of this method the dates of Great Zimbabwe have been pinponted, and even allowing a slight margin for error, these reinforce the findings of archaeologists, Dr David Randall-MacIver and Dr Gertrude Caton-Thompson, earlier this century.

Great Zimbabwe was built from 1100 AD and was in decline by 1450 AD prior to abandonment in about 1500 AD.

It was not built in biblical times and did not fall because of 19th century Nguni invasions. It existed between these events.

Radiocarbon dating originates from the development of nuclear weapons in the Second World War. It measures the chemical disintegration of radioactive particles caused by interaction between the sun's rays and earthly items such as the charcoal, bones and timber used at Great Zimbabwe.

Great Enclosure: *Imba Huru*

Of all the areas at the monument, the Great Enclosure is the most hypnotic. There, as one wanders through the tumbled masonry, towering walls, narrow passageways, and gazes at the Conical Tower, the imagination can easily run riot.

Why was this magnificent monument built? Who lived here? What does the Conical Tower represent? Why was it all abandoned? Unfortunately, we cannot answer all these questions. Some of Great Zimbabwe's mysteries are secure for all time and perhaps that is the way the occupants would have wished it.

But what do we know when fact and fiction are separated? Immediately, and visually, it is obvious that the Great Enclosure represents the crowning achievement for the builders of Great Zimbabwe.

This is the largest stone structure in Africa south of the Pyramids in Eygpt. Chief Mugabe's people call it *Imba Huru*, the Great House. While that tends to be descriptively sparing, a great house it certainly is, imposing and enormous.

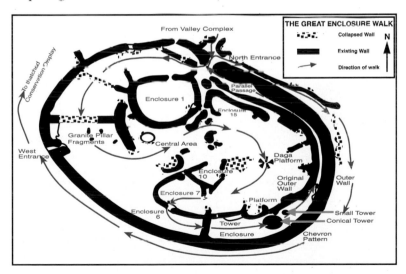

The visitor enters the Great Enclosure along a narrow buttressed, sunken passageway, one of five paths which converge at the north entrance. It is easy to speculate as one navigates the pathway that this

Great Enclosure wall with chevron design at top.

was part of ensuring privacy and the screening out of unwanted visitors for those who lived in the Great Enclosure.

Once inside the Great Enclosure, move anti-clockwise past tumbled inner walls to the broken fragments of four granite pillars. The largest once stood four metres high, and the pillars were favoured by early white settlers to sit or lean against to have their pictures taken.

Keep moving on in a circular manner bearing to your left just inside the reconstructed West Entrance. You will pass through a narrow gap in the wall ahead of you to enter the heart of the Great Enclosure.

The central part of the Great Enclosure is more tumbledown than the outer sections. This is because of the area's greater antiquity. Rather like most buildings today, a central unit is built first, then added to. Thus the outer enclosure came last, the inner enclosures at least a century before, and the abodes in the centre even earlier.

Away from the outer wall, there is a raised platform joined on either side by the original outer wall. Slightly to the left there is a small tower, and to the right, the Tower Enclosure.

Both sides of the walled entrance to the Tower Enclosure are decorated with black lines of schist. The variations between the masonry used on the existing outer wall and the old outer wall are clearly visible.

Near the raised platform there is a *daga* mound, surrounded by modern fencing and covered by a thatched structure. These modern structures are to protect the weathered mound of *daga* from the environment and visitors.

Thatched structure protects *daga* mound.

The inner enclosure, which may have been the original building, lies further across the Great Enclosure from the Conical Tower. It is approached through two facing entrances traversing a narrow pasage.

This circular wall is believed to have been where another household lived.

On your right is a large semi-circular platform, elevated and projecting from the wall behind. Its function is a matter of speculation, one theory being that it served as the throne of the senior wife or queen.

Behind it lies the Conical Tower. Apart from the outer wall, the elliptical tower is Great Zimbabwe's most imposing and photogenic standing structure. It is five metres in diameter at the base, two metres in diameter at its beehive-shaped summit, and ten metres high.

The Conical Tower.

There were two lines of "dentelle" ornament surrounding the top. But these have now disappeared and the shape of the original top of the Conical Tower above these is uncertain.

Over many decades rumours have abounded that the tower hid a secret treasure chamber. It has been prodded and probed, tunnelled underneath, and no mysteries have been revealed. It has only been proved that it is filled with stones like the walls.

So what was its purpose? Here we can only speculate. Did it represent a Shona grain storage bin, male authority, or the ruler himself?

It was one of the last structures to be built at Great Zimbabwe, the final achievement of the stone masons who took hundreds of years to build the whole monument. Could it be that they constructed it as a testimony to their endeavours rather as today roof wettings are held as a building nears completion?

Flanked by two of the four surviving muchechete edible fruit trees remaining in the Great Enclosure, the Conical Tower stands like a mighty and silent sentinal, defying all attempts to explain its secrets.

Leaving the Conical Tower behind you now enter the Parallel Passage. At its narrowest, only one person can pass through at a time, and you will quickly understand how easy it would have been to protect the persons living inside the wall. You will also notice how cool it is.

The inner wall on your left is at least a century older than the outer wall, and stones have been placed along the floor of the narrow passageway so that you do not have to plough through a sea of mud in the wet season.

The passage is 70 metres long and in places only 80 cm wide. Those given access would have taken part in ceremonies in the Conical Tower area, but would have been denied access to the living quarters.

Six well-preserved drains are still visible above the level of the path in the walls of the passage and by peering through these you will observe the thickness of the Outer Wall.

At the end of the Parallel Passage you leave through the Northern Entrance. You climb a short flight of six outside steps which are original and are of a completely unique local design.

Now you bear right along another narrow passageway which takes you to the magnificent Outer Wall with its chevron patterns.

The wall is 11 metres at its highest point and is six metres deep at the thickest part. The finest shaped stones were used in its construction and on the top of the wall a number of elongated pillars project skywards.

Just below the top of the wall there are two zig-zag bands in a chevron pattern. This is one of Great Zimbabwe's most distinctive and decorative features frequently used by designers today.

As one moves around the wall towards the Western Entrance the visitor can only regard with awe the builders' achievements.

Moving around the wall the visitor comes to the West Entrance. This has been reconstructed because the wall was bulging and in danger of collapsing. Like all granite walls, seen on a smaller scale in farms in Europe and North America, these walls need maintenance, and part of the reason why much of the monument is in a tumbled state is because they were not maintained.

But, with qualified archaeologists now in charge of restoration at Great Zimbabwe, the work is being much more carefully and painstakingly done than it was even in the early years after independence in 1980.

If the visitor looks carefuly at areas where walls are obviously bulging, they will see tiny, discreet, spots of paint. These are colour coded, so that if a wall has to be rebuilt, each stone is laid back in its original place.

Such restoration occurred at the West Entrance, and this work revealed one exciting and important find which further confirmed the date of Great Zimbabwe and the usage of local materials.

Among the stones, traces of the original wooden lintel were found. These wooden splinters were carbon dated and analysed. These scientific tests put the date of the timber at 1115 +/- 73 AD and confirmed it was a local hardwood, not an imported cedar as Mauch had speculated.

Once outside the Western Entrance, it is well worth looking back at the outer wall to comprehend its enormity. It is 255 metres in circumference, incorporating a million granite blocks, weighing some 15,000 tonnes.

To your left, the blocks are poorly matched and uneven. There are also greater numbers of small wedges between the stones where the builders have filled in gaps to hold the structure together. These wedges are particular problem areas with the walls less stable where they are inserted.

As the building of the wall proceeded towards the east, the builders' skills improved, and one sees the progression from P to Q construction.

Just outside the West Entrance there is a small thatch-covered Conservation Centre which explains the rehabilitation work which was done to the West Entrance.

Thereafter, you are ready to move on to the museum which houses the Zimbabwe Birds.

ZIMBABWE BIRDS

The competition for political authenticity through association with the Zimbabwe Bird has been occurring for over a century and is most vividly illustrated in its usage by the Southern Rhodesian white settlers — and subequently by African nationalists.

From 1932 to 1955, and again from 1964 to Zimbabwe's birth and independence in 1980, the Zimbabwe Bird appeared on the Southern Rhodesian coat of arms and currency.

Prior to 1932, Southern Rhodesia had used British coins which ceased to be legal tender on 8 July 1939. The first Southern Rhodesian silver one-shilling coin carried an impression of the Zimbabwe Bird on the reverse side.

The nine-year break from 1955 to 1964 occurred during the Federation of Rhodesia and Nyasaland when a common Federal currency replaced those of the three countries. The first new Southern Rhodesian coins, still bearing the Zimbabwe Bird on the reverse side, but now on the florin, were minted in 1964 after the break-up of the Federation.

After independence in 1980, the Zimbabwe Bird was elevated from the reverse to the front of coins and appeared on all of them.

The Zimbabwe National Party (ZNP), formed in June 1961, is thought to have been the first black nationalist political movement to use Zimbabwe in its title.

The ZNP swiftly faded from the scene with the December

Names

During the colonial era foreign names were given to different areas of the Ruins. These have been changed since independence and for clarity the new names, with the colonial name listed in brackets, are given below:

Central Valley (Posselt and Phillips Ruins)
Eastern Valley (Maund Ruin)
Eastern Ridge (Mauch Ruin)
Hill Complex (Acropolis)
Western Valley (Renders Ruin)

The Zimbabwe Birds recovered from the Ruins are carved from soapstone (steatite), a soft and easy-to-work, grey-greenish rock widely found in Zimbabwe where stone sculpture remains a highly popular and profitable occupation.

They measure 1.5 metres to 1.75 metres overall, 28 cm being the Bird above the pedestal. The Zimbabwe Bird used on the flag and other national symbols was the only one not recovered from the Hill Complex having been found in the Valley Complex.

The meaning and usage of the Zimbabwe Birds falls into the realm of speculation. But they have been linked to birds, notably the

The last Zimbabwe Bird found by Hall in 1903.

Bateleur and Fish Eagles, and animals, or both, which feature in Shona religious beliefs and practices. The crocodile motif on one of the Birds is associated with royalty.

So great is the symbolism of the Zimbabwe Bird that it is used as a logo by many commercial companies in Zimbabwe, as well as featuring on the flag, coat of arms, national anthem, coins, and as the watermark of notes.

1961 formation of the Zimbabwe African People's Union (ZAPU). Almost two years later, a group of leaders broke away to form the Zimbabwe African National Union (ZANU). Both movements, which spearheaded the country's fight against settler domination, used the word Zimbabwe in the names of their guerrilla armies.

Rhodes was obsessed by Great Zimbabwe and the Zimbabwe Birds. The Bird he purchased was mounted on a plinth at his Groote Schuur home in Cape Town, now the residence of the South African Vice President, where it remains. Rhodes gave plaster replicas of it to friends, and he had larger replicas made and mounted on the gateposts of his English home near Cambridge.

Mathematically, the numbers of Zimbabwe Birds known to have existed and to have been returned to

Zimbabwe do not seem to add up. It probably does not matter how many there were for the numbers we may argue about today are almost certainly fewer than existed at the height of Great Zimbabwe.

Zimbabwe Birds that were returned from South Africa after independence.

Authentic artefacts

Many of the artefacts, particularly those you will see in hotels, lodges and curio shops, are not authentic to the area. Whether this has occurred because of ignorance by the interior decorators, or because the non-local items sell better, is unclear.

So that the visitor is not misled by the artefacts they see, the following inventory lists some Shona/Karanga traditional arts and crafts found in the area, their uses, and gives the Shona name in brackets.

Functional pottery: Small, medium, large and very large cooking pots are used to cook relish *(chikari)*, sadza *(shambakodzi)*, beer *(gate)* and pumpkins and mealies *(rongo)*. A beer or milk serving pot *(chipfuko)* is decorated while there are two types of storage pots *(nyengero* and *denhe)* for beer and milk respectively. A broken half pot *(chaenga)* is used for roasting nuts.

Archaeological pottery: Includes zoomorphic (in the form of an animal) pottery found near Great Zimbabwe. The pottery comes in different shapes and sizes and is decorated with various motifs.

Wooden artefacts: Includes functional items such as a mortar and pestle, a small mortar *(whedza)* for milking cows, cooking sticks of three types and cooking spoons.

Basketware: Comes in various shapes and sizes, the largest being called *dengu*.

Musical instruments: The most common are the thumb piano *(mbira)*; a cross between a guitar and violin often fashioned from a gourd with a single string *(chipendani)*; various sized and shaped drums *(ngoma)* which may be decorated; leg jingles *(magavu)*; hand jingles *(hosho)*; and horns *(hwamanda)* usually from a kudu, are the most common.

Hunting weapons: Includes bows *(uta)* and arrows *(miseve)*, spears *(pfumo)*, clubs *(tsvimbo)* and nets *(mambure)* for trapping game. Fighting weapons have similar names and these include the battle axe *(gano)* and machete *(bakatwa)*.

Religious and ceremonial artefacts: These include crescent-shaped axes, spears, divining dice *(hakata)* and walking sticks *(mudonzvo)* which may be decorated with a snake or crocodile.

The above list is not exhaustive. It is simply intended to give you some guidance as to artefacts which are authentic to the Great Zimbabwe area. Thereafter, you must trust your judgement or the advice you are given.

MASVINGO

In August 1890 the "Pioneer Column" of 117 wagons and 180 "Pioneers", fearful of provoking the Ndebele, skirted Matabeleland, and finally found a way through the hills thereby opening their gateway to the plains of Mashonaland. They called the access Providential Pass.

At a place called Isakata, named after nearby hills, they hoisted the British flag and began building the first settler town which they called Fort Victoria after the distant British monarch.

In her book, *A Town Called Victoria*, Katherine Sayce frankly and brutally spells out the reasons why the town was created:

Mashonaland "...was reputedly richly endowed with minerals and so, like any other African territory in the late nineteenth century with such a reputation, it was due for European domination, exploitation and civilisation".

Cars outside Fort Victoria Hotel.

Rhodes contracted a 23-year-old adventurer, Frank Johnson, to drive a wagon road from Bechuanaland (now Botswana) to Mount Hampden (initially the site of Salisbury, renamed Harare in 1980), and build forts along the route to protect prospectors and other civilians.

The original Fort Victoria, later moved to the present site because of disease and inadaquate water, was located on a farm just off the Beitbridge road. It was the first fort on the way to Mount Hampden.

It was to be a crossroad for longer journeys, but it was not much to write home about, and the mail was highly unreliable.

The town comprised a 60-foot square fort with five-foot-high earthworks surrounded by a shallow ditch. There were rifle slits and a mount for a Gatling-gun to fight off the Ndebele.

Today the town is called Masvingo. Its two main streets lead to Harare, to Birchenough Bridge and the Eastern Highlands, and to Beitbridge, the gateway to and from South Africa. It is equidistant from Zimbabwe's main cities, and then, as now, it is a crossroad, and a place to pause for those visiting Great Zimbabwe.

"Masvingo isn't bad for an hour or so strolling around the centre," the author of one guide writes. "That is an exaggeration," said one local resident, "five minutes is enough!" Other residents, as one might expect, strenuously object to such judgements, believing Masvingo to be the hub of the region.

The town's first newspaper, launched on 11 November 1890, was called *The Nugget*. Many of the residents were prospectors pegging claims through the area and relying on local African produce to supplement their diets.

"Few settlers were at this stage, or for many years afterwards, farming the land, despite reports reaching the south that the area was admirably suited to such enterprise," Sayce wrote.

But gradually, as it was realised that the area was not richly endowed with minerals, the settlers moved into farming and commerce.

Today, Masvingo, Zimbabwe's sixth largest city, is endeavouring to break out of the underdevelopment which has dogged it. It is actively trying to attract investors through a glossy brochure which promises "No Red Tape, Lots of Red Carpet".

For the visitor the main attractions lie outside Masvingo. Great Zimbabwe currently attracts some 100,000 visitors a year. Lake Mutirikwi is noted for its bass fishing and water sports, and the 8,900-hectare Lake Kyle National Park is the one place in Zimbabwe where the visitor is almost assured of seeing white rhino in the wild.

Beyond that its only claim to fame is that it was Southern Rhodesia's first white settler town.

WHERE TO STAY

Your choices are limited. In Masvingo town itself, the three hotels are the Flamboyant, Chevron, and the Masvingo A1. None of them are recommended although the first two say they are refurbishing their premises — and image.

There are no restaurants for the visitor, although food can be obtained at filling stations such as Ace Motors in town, which serves good basic food and Shell City on the Beitbridge road. They offer the advantage of filling your car and stomach at the same place which takes care of two of your needs. The Roselli Gallery serves light snacks as well as exhibiting sculpture and paintings.

There are a few basic backpackerish places in Masvingo. But if you are looking for a bed for the night you are better off travelling to the Great Zimbabwe area which is what brings most visitors to the area in the first place.

At the monument the only hotel is the Great Zimbabwe Hotel run by Zimbabwe Sun Hotels. The rooms are comfortable and the dining room offers a wide choice. There are cheap family rooms and room rates vary at different times of the year.

Nearby is the Lodge at the Ancient City which is a welcome addition to the area. The hospitality and rooms are expansive and the food is recommended by the lodges visitors. Provides guided tours of the area including to Great Zimbabwe and Kyle Recreational Park.

Karanga Lodge, a two-storey house converted into a lodge, on the shore of Lake Mutirikwi, is marginally cheaper than the Ancient City, and there are a number of self-catering facilities, as well as five camping sites in the area, the most popular of which is at Great Zimbabwe. Sunbird Safaris conducts tours in the area.

For those who want wildlife as well as ruins, there are two alternatives. One is the self-catering National Park facility in Kyle National Park

An ostrich at Pa-Nyanda.

where booking should be made well in advance, particularly in school holidays.

The other is Pa-Nyanda Lodge, 11 km south of Masvingo, just off the main road from Beitbridge. Set on a 5,000-acre game and ostrich farm, the lodge has an excellent dry season waterhole in front, comfortable family accommodation, and is all-inclusive or self-catering.

Further afield, along Murray MacDougal Drive, is the Glenlivet and self-catering Hippo Hotel.

Places of Interest
Apart from Great Zimbabwe and the Kyle Recreational Park, where you are almost assured of seeing white rhino, from horseback or your vehicle, the places of interest for tourists to the area are limited.

On Masvingo's main street there is the Bell Tower which formed one of the corners of the original Fort Victoria from which it was transfered. Just outside town on the Birchenough

White rhino at Kyle Recreational Park.

Bridge road (which leads to Mutare) there is a chapel built by Italian prisoners interned in Rhodesia during the Second World War.

Bondolfi, Serima and Driefontein Missions produce fine leather work, wooden carvings and artwork, and curios can be obtained at the Warthog Curio Shop at Shell City, at various roadside markets, and near the town centre.

Lake Mutirikwi and dam wall.

Lake Mutirikwi has boating and fishing. There is a scenic drive along Murray MacDougal Drive which passes the dam wall, colourfully painted houses in the communal lands, and the mountainous Glenlivet area. This route rejoins the road to Mutare.

There is a low grade hospital, pharmacies, plenty of 24-hour petrol stations, a publicity bureau, banks, churches of many denominations, a mosque, a nine-hole golf course and sports club. Belmont Press is the best place for books, magazines and newspapers.

On the road from Harare to Masvingo there are two stopovers fairly near to Masvingo. The first is Denise's Kitchen 156 km from Harare. Light meals are available, there is a curio shop and some wildlife wandering the fenced lawns. Accomodation in thatched chalets is available as are elephant rides, game drives and horse riding at the nearby, affiliated Tangenhamo Safaris.

The Golden Spiderweb, 222 km from Harare and 70 km before Masvingo, also serves light meals and is a good place to shop for crochet, embroidery and other souvenirs.

CHECKLIST OF BIRDS OF GREAT ZIMBABWE

All numbers used are taken from Roberts' *Birds of Southern Africa*. This list was compiled by Dr Kit Hustler of Wild Horizons, PO Box 159, Victoria Falls, Zimbabwe (Tel: 263 (13) 4219) and Mr Peter Ginn of Peter Ginn Birding Safaris, PO Box 44, Marondera, Zimbabwe (Tel/Fax: 263 (79) 23411). This is not a definitive list of the 350 bird species to be found in the area but a general guide to what can be seen by those wandering through the Ruins and surrounding bushveld.

No.	Bird Name	No.	Bird Name
008	Dabchick	209	Crowned Crane
055	Whitebreasted Cormorant	213	Black Crake
058	Reed Cormorant	226	Moorhen
060	Darter	228	Redknobbed Coot
062	Grey Heron	230	Kori Bustard
063	Blackheaded Heron	240	African Jacana
066	Great White Egret	249	Threebanded Plover
067	Little Egret	255	Crowned Plover
071	Cattle Egret	258	Blacksmith Plover
081	Hamerkop	260	Wattled Plover
083	White Stork	266	Wood Sandpiper
085	Abdim's Stork	297	Spotted Dikkop
088	Saddlebill Stork	298	Water Dikkop
091	Sacred Ibis	315	Greyheaded Gull
101	Whitebacked Duck	349	Rock Pigeon
102	Egyptian Goose	352	Redeyed Dove
105	African Black Duck	354	Cape Turtle Dove
108	Redbilled Teal	355	Laughing Dove
115	Knobbilled Duck	356	Namaqua Dove
116	Spurwinged Goose	358	Greenspotted Dove
118	Secretary Bird	361	Green Pigeon
123	Whitebacked Vulture	371	Purplecrested Lourie
126a	Yellowbilled Kite	373	Grey Lourie
127	Blackshouldered Kite	377	Redchested Cuckoo
131	Black Eagle	381	Striped Cuckoo
132	Tawny Eagle	382	Jacobin Cuckoo
135	Wahlberg's Eagle	386	Diederik Cuckoo
142	Brown Snake Eagle	390	Senegal Coucal
143	Blackbreasted Snake Eagle	394	Wood Owl
146	Bateleur	395	Marsh Owl
148	African Fish Eagle	398	Pearlspotted Owl
149	Steppe Buzzard	401	Spotted Eagle Owl
154	Lizard Buzzard	402	Giant Eagle Owl
169	Gymnogene	417	Little Swift
172	Lanner Falcon	421	Palm Swift
180	E. Redfooted Kestrel	426	Redfaced Mousebird
196	Natal Francolin	428	Pied Kingfisher
199	Swainson's Francolin	429	Giant Kingfisher
203	Helmeted Guinea Fowl	431	Malachite Kingfisher

No.	Bird Name	No.	Bird Name
435	Brownhooded Kingfisher	701	Chinspot Batis
438	European Bee-eater	710	Paradise Flycatcher
443	Whitefronted Bee-eater	711	African Pied Wagtail
444	Little Bee-eater	713	Cape Wagtail
446	European Roller	727	Orangethroated Longclaw
447	Lilacbreasted Roller	728	Yellowthroated Longclaw
448	Rackettailed Roller	732	Fiscal Shrike
449	Purple Roller	733	Redbacked Shrike
450	Broadbilled Roller	735	Longtailed Shrike
451	Hoopoe	737	Tropical Boubou
452	Redbilled Woodhoopoe	740	Puffback
454	Scimitarbilled Woodhoopoe	753	White Helmet Shrike
455	Trumpeter Hornbill	756	Whitecrowned Shrike
457	Grey Hornbill	761	Plumcoloured Starling
458	Redbilled Hornbill	765	Greater Blue-eared Starling
460	Crowned Hornbill	769	Redwinged Starling
463	Ground Hornbill	784	Miombo Doublecollared
464	Blackcollared Barbet		Sunbird
470	Yellowfronted Tinker Barbet	786	Yellowbellied Sunbird
473	Crested Barbet	787	Whitebellied Sunbird
486	Cardinal Woodpecker	791	Scarletchested Sunbird
494	Rufousnaped Lark	792	Black Sunbird
496	Flappet Lark	797	Yellow White-Eye
518	European Swallow	798	Redbill Buffalo Weaver
522	Wiretailed Swallow	799	Whitebrowed Sparrowweaver
524	Redbreasted Swallow	801	House Sparrow
527	Lesserstriped Swallow	804	Greyheaded Sparrow
529	Rock Martin	805	Yellowthroated Sparrow
531	Greyrumped Swallow	811	Spottedbacked Weaver
541	Forktailed Drongo	814	Masked Weaver
544	African Golden Oriole	816	Golden Weaver
545	Blackheaded Oriole	819	Redheaded Weaver
547	Black Crow	821	Redbilled Quelea
548	Pied Crow	824	Red Bishop
550	Whitenecked Raven	827	Yellowrumped Widow
560	Arrowmarked Babbler	829	Whitewinged Widow
568	Blackeyed Bulbul	830	Yellowbacked Widow
576	Kurrichane Thrush	831	Redcollared Widow
580	Groundscraper Thrush	844	Blue Waxbill
587	Capped Wheatear	846	Common Waxbill
593	Mocking Chat	860	Pintailed Whydah
596	Stone Chat	862	Paradise Whydah
599	Heuglin's Robin	865	Purple Widowfinch
645	Barthroated Apalis	869	Yelloweye Canary
672	Rattling Cisticola	870	Blackthroated Canary
683	Tawnyflanked Prinia	881	Streakyheaded Canary
689	Spotted Flycatcher	884	Goldenbreasted Bunting
694	Black Flycatcher	886	Rock Bunting

CHECKLIST OF TREES AND SHRUBS OF GREAT ZIMBABWE

The following checklist includes some of the more common, or more notable, trees and shrubs to be seen in and around Great Zimbabwe. Meg Coate Palgrave's *Key to the Trees of Zimbabwe* is recommended. In addition, the "Know Your Trees" course provides unique insights. Bookings: PO Box 4643, Harare, Zimbabwe (Tel: 263 (4) 742 765 Fax: 263 (4) 742 800)

Tree/Shrub Name	Botanical Name
Broad-Leaved Erythrina	Erythrina latissima
Broom-Cluster Fig	Ficus sur
Buffalo-Thorn	Ziziphus mucronata
Cabbage Tree	Cussonia spicata
Candelabra Tree	Euphorbia ingens
Common Red Milkwood	Mimusops zeyheri
Common Wild Fig	Ficus thonningii
Excelsa	Aloe excelsa
Giant-Leaved Fig	Ficus lutea
Ginger Bush	Tetradenia riparia
Grey Grewia	Grewia monticola
Large-Leaved Rock Fig	Ficus abutilifolia
Lavender Croton	Croton gratissimus
Lavender Tree	Heteropyxis dehniae
Lucky Bean Tree	Erythrina lysistemon
Mobola Plum	Parinari curatellifolia
Monkeybread	Piliostigma thonningii
Mukwa	Pterocarpus angolensis
Munondo	Julbernardia globiflora
Musasa	Brachystegia spiciformis
Paperbark Acacia	Acacia sieberiana
Paperbark Commiphora	Commiphora marlothii
Pittosporum	Pittosporum viridiflorum
Powder-Bark Gardenia	Gardenia ternifolia
Red-Hot-Poker Tree	Erythrina abyssinica
Round-Leaved Bloodwood	Pterocarpus rotundifolius
Sickle Bush	Dichrostachys cinerea
Silver Terminalia	Terminalia sericea
Snuggle-Leaf	Pouzolzia mixta
Spiny Monkey Orange	Strychnos spinosa
Stem-Fruit	Englerophyton magalismontanum
Twin-Berry Tree	Oricia bachmannii
Velvet Leaved Combretum	Combretum molle
White Cat's Whiskers	Clerodendrum glabrum
White Thorn-Tree	Acacia polyacantha
Wild Pear	Dombeya rotundifolia
Wild Wisteria	Bolusanthus speciosus
Wing-Leaved Wooden Pear	Schrebera alata
Winter Senna	Senna singueana
Yellow Brachylena	Brachylaena rotundata

Further reading

A large amount has been written about Great Zimbabwe and much of it belongs in the fantasy world. Some early treasure hunters' writing contains fragments of importance. Only the main scientific and serious works on Great Zimbabwe and affiliated subjects are recomended here:

Beach, D., *The Shona of Zimbabwe: 900 -1850,* Heinemann and Mambo Press, Zimbabwe, 1980.

Caton-Thompson, G., *The Zimbabwe Culture: Ruins and Reactions,* UK, 1931.

Garlake, P., *Great Zimbabwe,* Thames and Hudson, UK, 1973.

Garlake, P., *Life at Great Zimbabwe,* Mambo Press, Zimbabwe, 1982.

Garlake, P., *Great Zimbabwe Described and Explained,* Zimbabwe Publishing House, Zimbabwe, 1982.

Garlake, P., *The Hunter's Vision: The Prehistoric Art of Zimbabwe,* Zimbabwe Publishing House and British Museum Press, 1995.

Malenga, E., *The Soapstone Birds of Great Zimbabwe,* African Publishing Group, Zimbabwe, 1997.

Mudenge, S.I.G., *A Political History of Munhumutapa c 1400-1902,* Zimbabwe Publishing House, Zimbabwe, 1988.

Randall-MacIver, D. R., *Mediaeval Rhodesia,* MacMillan, UK, 1906.

Summers, R., *Ancient Ruins and Vanished Civilisations of Southern Africa,* Bulpin, South Africa, 1971.

Thomas, A., *Rhodes: The Race for Africa,* Zimbabwe Publishing House, Zimbabwe and BBC Books, 1996.

Meshack Asare's award-winning children's book, *Chipo and the Bird on the Hill: A tale of ancient Zimbabwe,* Zimbabwe Publishing House, 1984, is both imaginative and beautifully illustrated by the author.

INDEX